Play Like A Legend
Bill Monroe Tunes & Songs for Mandolin
by Joe Carr

Cover photo: Right to left; Vic Jordan, Bill Monroe, Roland White
Sunset Park, West Grove, Pennsylvania, 1968. Photograph by Artie Rose. Used by permission.

CD track listing

Contents

Titles are followed by year of recording and key of performance. Special thanks to Gerald Jones for his playing on the CD and to Artie Rose for the use of his unique photographs.

 EADG Tuning Notes

BARNES & NOBLE

www.bn.com

Sold To:
Frank Montague
14591 Leary St
Nokesville, VA 20181
USA

Ship To:
Frank Montague
14591 Leary St
Nokesville, VA 20181
USA

Customer Service:
1-800-THE-BOOK
service@barnesandnoble.com

PO Num: 1163490371

Loc: PM0203
Box Size: NK1

Your order of Jan 01, 2014 **(Order No. 708345149)**

Qty	Description	Item #	Item Price	Total
1	**Play Like A Legend Book/CD Set**	9780786683581	26.99	26.99

If you are not satisfied with your order, you may return it within 14 days of the delivery date. For your convenience, items may be returned to the address on the packing slip or returned to your local Barnes & Noble store (check the local store refund policy for details).

Choose a return reason below and include this slip with the item in your package. Please cut out label on dotted line and affix to carton being returned.

[ ] **Wrong Quantity**

[ ] **Defective or Damaged in Transit**

[ ] **Wrong Merchandise Received**

[ ] **Other (please explain)**_____

Credit Card#: **

Pay Method: GC

From:
Frank Montague
14591 Leary St
Nokesville, VA 20181
USA

To:
**Barnes & Noble.com
B&N.COM Customer Returns
1 Barnes & Noble Way
Monroe Township, NJ 08831**
USA

708345149

THANK YOU FOR YOUR ORDER!

Please note sales tax for the state of VA was collected on this order.

9905000000811430125

01/02/2014 12:00 AM   (CL)

01/02/2014 6:16 PM   (PRINT)

Page 1 of 1

Play Like a Legend: Bill Monroe Tunes and Songs for Mandolin

This volume is designed to introduce intermediate to advanced mandolin players to the Monroe mandolin style using a variety of essential concepts, techniques and instructive tunes. The material here includes transcriptions of solos played by Bill Monroe from the 1940s to the 1990s. Several features that define Monroe's style as a unique approach are explained. It is hoped that the student can take these concepts and apply them to new material. Also included are several tunes never recorded by Monroe arranged as he might have approached this material. An additional special feature of this work is the sixteen pages of previously unpublished photogaphs of Bill Monroe, his band and special musical guests taken in the 1960s and 70s. These photographs are taken from a huge archive of pictures taken by self-described bluegrass fan, Artie Rose. Mr. Rose has graciously agreed to allow this material to be published here. Monroe fans will no doubt find these photos to be rare and enjoyable glimpses into the past.

Known as *The Father of Bluegrass Music,* Bill Monroe has received much deserved credit as the innovator of the new music form called bluegrass. As a bandleader, often through difficult times, he led his band the Bluegrass Boys from 1939 until his death in 1996. During this extended period (57 years!,) he attracted a who's who of great musicians to his band who defined the genre in its first and second generations. As the developer of the music, he experimented through trial and rejection until he found the perfect instrumental mix for his new music. As a song and tune writer, he developed a massive repertoire that literally defined the style. As the father figure of the music, he struck a huge image of a proud independent man uncompromised by the fads of the day.

Despite all these admirable roles, it is as a mandolin player that Monroe has received the least general acclaim. Writers never identified Monroe's mandolin playing nor sung its praises the way they did with other instrumentalists. This may be because reviewers who are not musicians are less able to comment on his unique contributions to the instrument. To this author, Monroe's contributions and impact on the mandolin's role in bluegrass music are no less iconic than that of Earl Scruggs and his well-documented impact on the 5-string banjo. Monroe took a gentle parlor instrument and created a powerful new lead voice capable of standing shoulder to shoulder with the other great instrumental voices of bluegrass. Through his development of specific licks, new techniques and tunes created for the instrument, he invented the unique vocabulary of bluegrass mandolin. These new mandolin ideas will forever be identified as "Monroe Style." Additionally he redefined the role of the mandolin as a rhythm instrument and gave it an important role as a powerful voice in the bluegrass band rhythm section.

Surprisingly, there has been no definitive work dedicated to Monroe's influential mandolin style. This work is an attempt to remedy that. The material here includes Monroe's approach to fiddle tunes, famous original instrumentals and Monroe's soloing approach to songs. Additionally, there are "in the style of" arrangements of tunes never recorded by Monroe.

Generally, the fiddle tune solos in the first section of this work could be considered the "easier" tunes. The song solos are presented in no particular order and the presentation is not meant to be in an order of increasing difficulty. Each solo contains its own set of techniques and licks worthy of intense study. An effort was made to avoid duplicating tunes in the Collins collection referenced at the end of this work.

The written page can only go so far to capture the essence of any musician. Focused, repeated listening to the enclosed CD, and especially the original recordings, is required to understand and replicate the powerful music here.

With the growing popularity of bluegrass music, entire generations of young mandolin players "skipped over" the Monroe style preferring to emulate more modern players. A lack of instructional materials detailing Monroe's style may partially account for this. These musicians may have studied fiddle inspired players only to discover these styles require exceptional technique and control - beyond the reach of many players. Modern Monroe-influenced players including Ricky Skaggs, Ronnie McCoury and Mike Compton show that the Monroe style is compelling and exciting to today's bluegrass fans. Well known players such as David Grisman and Sam Bush, who are not considered to be Monroe style players, effectively emulate Monroe when they want to. Additionally, and perhaps more importantly, Monroe's style is accessible to most players of even modest skill level. The approaches that served Monroe well into his 80s, are valuable skills that anyone can use to benefit their mandolin playing.

Monroe Style Mandolin

It is interesting (and instructive) to note here that throughout his career, Monroe gave credit to his Uncle Pen as a major influence on his developing style. Despite his lip service to his fiddling uncle, the evidence of Monroe's mandolin playing does not support this. Many mandolin players before and after Monroe looked with good reason to the fiddle for inspiration with satisfactory if uninspiring results. Monroe, however, realized that while the two instruments are tuned the same, many fiddle ideas simply do not translate well to the mandolin. The mandolin player uses a pick rather than a bow to produce notes. Players who view the mandolin as a "poor man's" fiddle were apt to see the pick as a serious limitation. Monroe used the pick to create new powerful ideas that did work well on the mandolin and were not native to the fiddle. Indeed, if Monroe had only followed the fiddle approach to mandolin playing, he likely would not have been notable as a mandolin player. By embracing the mandolin on its own terms and not simply as an extension of the fiddle, he was able to take advantage of many elements that make the mandolin unique.

How Does He Play So Fast?

Monroe was reportedly once asked this question. "I'm not fast, I'm quick" was his response. I have given this seemingly inscrutable response some thought since, although it was confusing to me, it apparently had meaning for him. After careful consideration, here are my thoughts: If *fast* means running a 100-yard dash and *quick* means catching a fly, Monroe may be saying that when he plays, producing each note is a short event done quickly like catching a fly. While others may look at the total 64 or so notes of the solo and try to play the entire series fast, Monroe may see the solo as a series of discreet events – each executed quickly. But how does all of this help a student play faster?

While there is no substitute for being innately talented or for having 60 plus years of experience, Monroe has several learnable techniques that allow him to play quickly. First (1), his right hand and wrist stay very relaxed even when playing at fast tempos. Watch internet videos of the master until you can readily "see" an image of his hand. Strive to emulate that relaxed position. Realize that your volume may be reduced when you first experiment with a loose wrist.

Second (2), his tune arrangements are designed for speed. Look at the transcription of *Turkey in the Straw*. Note the repeated notes throughout the A section. AND note that this entire section is played with the powerful 1, 2 and 3 fingers. Practice the G arpeggio/scale shape produced by the notes in the A section until they are second nature and your fingers move effortlessly to the frets. The fingers almost form the familiar G "chop" chord position as they hover over the fingerboard. By the time you have repeated this pattern 100,000 times, your hand will begin to recognize it as Monroe must have. See the notes for *Katy Hill* for a detailed explanation and practice examples.

Monroe, very likely, did not work out solos like this slowly. They were improvised at speed on stage. The patterns were so familiar that all the sounds were expected. There were no surprises in that G position. In your practice, strive for that familiarity.

Third (3), there are a number of common fiddle tune phrases that are difficult to play well on the mandolin at fast tempos. Monroe invented alterations of these phrases to create similar but vastly more playable licks. Examples are shown in the tune notes as they appear. Fourth (4), his unique note doubling technique allowed him to keep the eighth note feel while slowing the speed of the left hand. Examples appear in the tunes.

Pick Direction

On eighth note based fiddle tunes, Monroe generally followed the standard pick direction rules - down on the downbeat and up on the weak beat which means alternating strokes on series of eighth notes. The exception is when he plays song solos in a blusy, driving style. In these cases, Monroe often used a very stacatto, all down picking approach. This attack gives the music a very distinctive, aggressive quality.

Monroe Chords

Bill Monroe's contribution to rhythm mandolin should not be overlooked. Before he devised the "chop" style of rhythm mandolin in the 1940s, the mandolin had been a quiet and even delicate rhythm instrument. Just as he did with lead mandolin, Monroe redefined the rhythm mandolin role so it could stand tall with the bass, guitar, banjo and fiddle as an important voice in the rhythm section.

His innovation was a deceptively simple one. Rather than strum on all four beats as a guitar does, Monroe played an abrupt chord " chop" on beats 2 and 4. This back beat rhythm occurred with the guitar as it strummed the chord. It also was placed between the bass's notes which were played on beats 1 and 3. The result was similar to a snaredrum or high hat cymbal played on the "weak" or "and" beats of the measure.

To accentuate the "chop," Monroe used a unique set of chord shapes that fit the style well. The first chord on the left below is often called the long bluegrass chop chord. It was likely "discovered" by Monroe and he certainly popularized its use. Well known bluegrass mandolin player Roland White remembers learning this chord shape by watching Monroe on a 1950s Los Angeles television performance. In the days of live television and no recording devices, Roland had to learn quickly before the camera panned away!

There are 2 groups of three chords in the diagrams below. The first three are the 1, 4 and 5 chords in the key of G. The long G form will likely be the most difficult. Getting the little pinkie finger to stretch to the 7th fret will be a challenge at first. Slide the chord shape up the neck to make the chord easier to play. Since the name of the chord is on the first string, this chord placed as written at the third fret is G. If you place it two frets higher at the 5th fret, it will be an A chord. Moving the chord up the neck, we get G (3,) G♯ (4,) A (5,) B♭ (6,) B (7,) and C (8.) By playing the C and D shapes at the correct frets, you can play the 4 and 5 chords in each of these keys.

The second set of three chords are the 1, 4 and 5 chords in the key of D. Moving these shapes gives us D (5 second string,) E (6,) F (7,) F♯ (8) and G (9.) The Xs indicate strings that should be muted and the diamond shaped notes indicate root notes. To begin, the pick direction of the rhythm should be all downstrokes.

These chord shapes are also important to understand Monroe's solo style. Later in this work, many of the song solos are played "in the chop chord position." This will become clear as you play through the solos, but for now, learn these shapes and practice until moving between them is effortless.

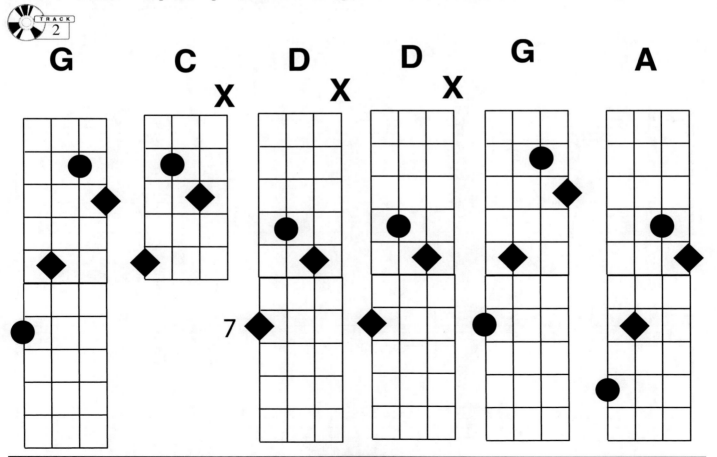

Rhythm Exercises

Below in exercise 1 is the basic Monroe rhythm chop. Begin on beat 1 (the rest) by placing your fingers over the required frets, but don't squeeze. On beat 2, squeeze and quickly release once the right hand has strummed the chord quickly and forcefully. Now get ready to repeat the action on beats 3 and 4. Squeeze and release the chord leaving your left hand fingers on the strings. Pat your foot to a count of four. "Chop" the chord on the "and" beats between the pats of your foot. If you are doing it right, the chop is done when the foot is in the air, between pats. The action is similar to that of a good swing style guitarist.

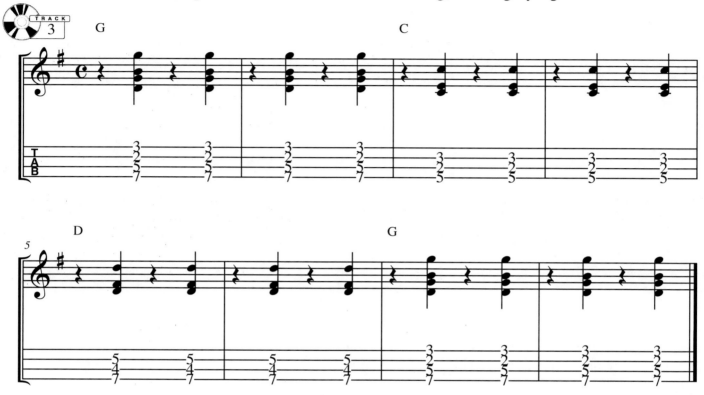

Monroe would occasionally start a song with a four beat rhythm like this. The chords on beats 2 and 4 are cut off short.

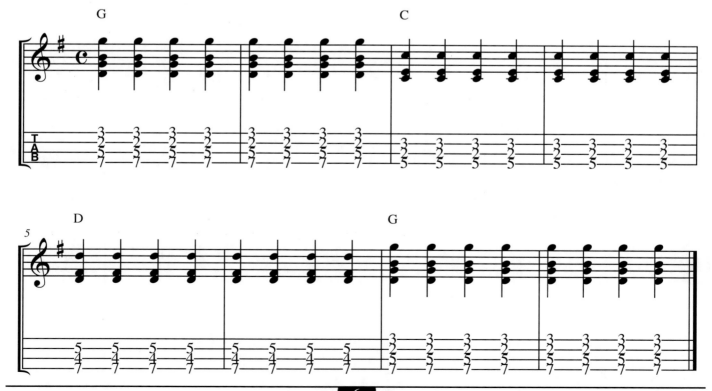

Boston Boy - traditional

Source: The Music of Bill Monroe- MCA Boxed Set - Here is a traditional fiddle tune in the key of C that demonstrates several of Monroe's approaches to such material. It was recorded quite late in hs career (1994) and is testament to his strength on the mandolin well into his later years. In measure 1, a fiddler likely would play a series of eight unique notes as in the example below.

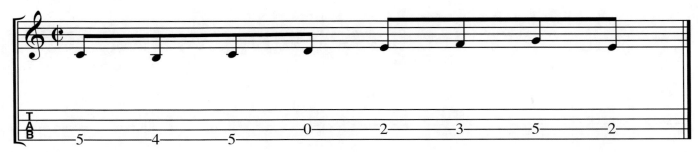

Look at Monroe's approach in measure 1 on the next page. Monroe slows the left hand movement with repeated notes while maintaining the eighth note flow. Note that measure 3 features the same fingering as measure 1 "moved over" one string.

Anticipation

In measure 8 under the first ending bracket, Monroe anticipates the repeat of the A part with two eighth note Cs at the end of the measure. He repeats this anticipation under the second ending bracket with the two eighth note Es moving into the B part. *Anticipation* is an important technique in bluegrass. The musician plays an upcoming note before it "belongs" or is expected. In *Boston Boy,* the anticipated notes occur one beat before the repeat of the A section and one beat before the B section. Anticipation gives the solo an agressive *forward leaning* feel – very common in bluegrass music. Look for anticipation throughout this volume.

Monroe's Musical Idiosycracies

As a soloist, Monroe took liberties that likely caused consternation in his other musicians but were tolerated as he was the bandleader. In American fiddle tune circles, for instance, the A part of the melody is normally played twice followed by two times through the B part. Monroe was no doubt aware of this convention. However, on recordings and in live performances, Monroe might break this unspoken rule by playing the B part first or some other non-standard approach to the tune. Because Monroe surrounded himself with superior musicians who listened for and reacted to such unusual solos, the band was able to play these tunes successfully without glitches. It is interesting that the other soloists played their solos in the standard way.

It has also been noted by several of Monroe's musicians that he would play a short chord "chop" to signal the key of the next song in the performance. Monroe did not prepare a set list for his shows, so the songs played might reflect his personal whim, an audience request or other influences. Since capoes were used by both the guitar and the banjo to play in various keys, Monroe's signal gave the musicians time to make adjustments while Monroe continued his introduction. This simple signal may have appeared to be a nervous tick to audience members, but it served as a valuable method of allowing the improvised show to progress without delay. Monroe was also known to start a song by simply beginning to play a rhythm chop on a static chord. Once the band joined him on the extended "vamp," Monroe would start singing the song.

Boston Boy

Source - The Music of Bill Monroe MCA Boxed Set - The A note in measures 2 and 6 requires a reach with the 4th finger. The slide in measure 13 is played with the 3rd finger. Play eighth notes with alternating pick strokes beginning each measure with a down and use downstrokes for the quarter notes. In measure 2, the seventh fret of A string is played with 4th or 3rd finger. When the phrase repeats in measure 6, shift to the third fret with the 1st finger until measure 7 where you can shift back to normal position during the open A note.

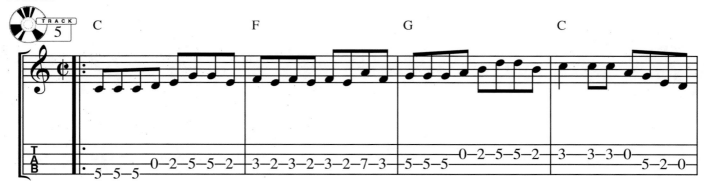

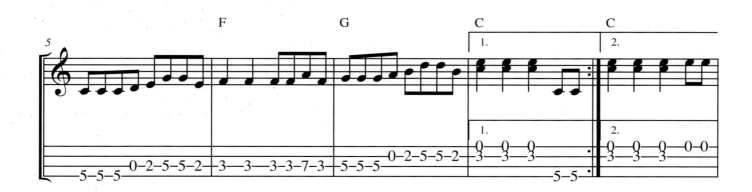

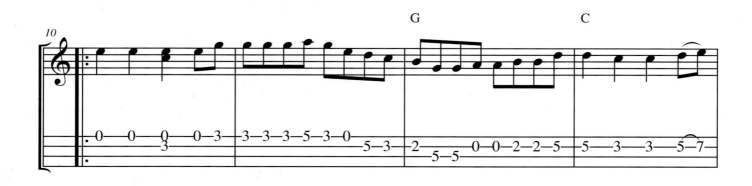

Salt Creek - Bill Monroe

Source - The Music of Bill Monroe MCA Boxed Set - This is a great first Monroe tune to learn. It is very popular in bluegrass jam sessions and this arrangement contains many of Monroe's signature soloing elements. Use the 3rd finger to slide in measure 10. This tune is known in some fiddle circles as "Salt River."

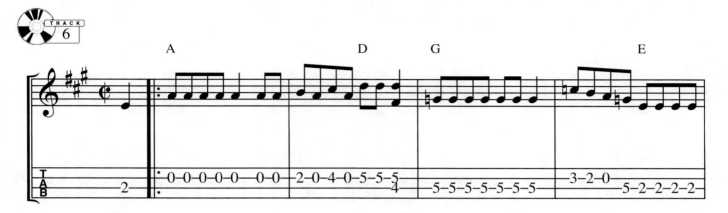

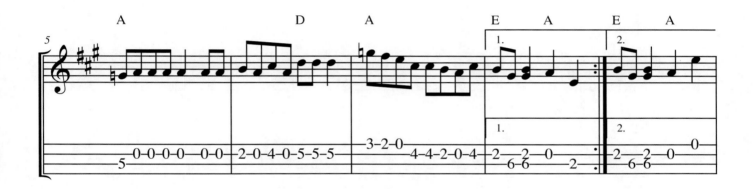

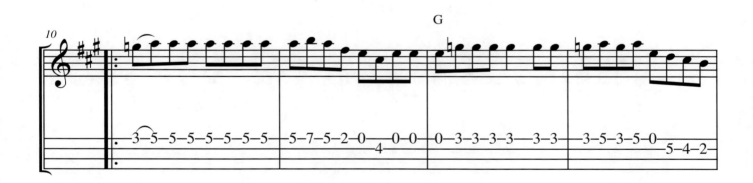

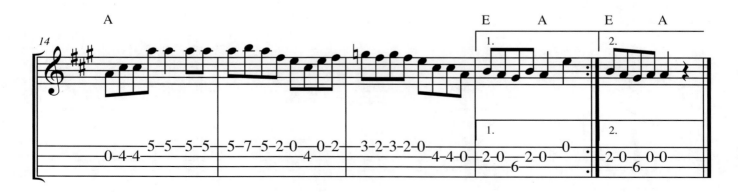

Cotton Eyed Joe - traditional

Source - Bill Monroe - Off The Record, Vol. 1: Live Recordings, 1956-1969, Smithsonian Folkways -This simple solo in A begins with one of Monroe's favorite rhythm figures – eighth, quarter, eighth, quarter, eighth, eighth played down, up, up, down, down, up. The A section only requires the 1st and 2nd fingers. The B section begins with the low 1-3-5 A major arpeggio which Monroe uses extensively in the key of A. Measure 12 introduces a bluesy lick using the C natural (flatted third) note.

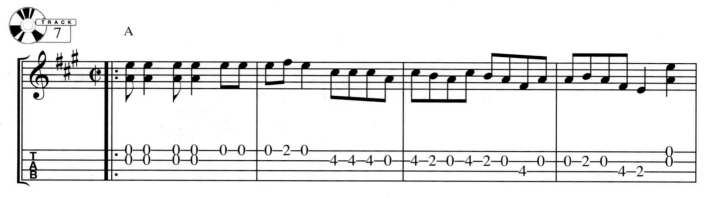

Dusty Miller - traditional

Source - The Music of Bill Monroe MCA Boxed Set – The eighth note approach here is broken by only a few quarter notes. Monroe uses a similar note set as in the A part of *Jerusalem Ridge* (A minor.) The slide in measure 9 & 13 can be fretted with the 2nd or 3rd finger. Because of the complex melody, this tune may be more challenging than the previous ones.

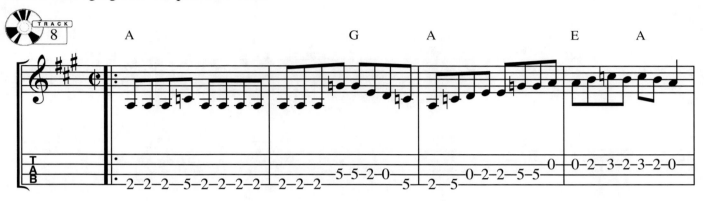

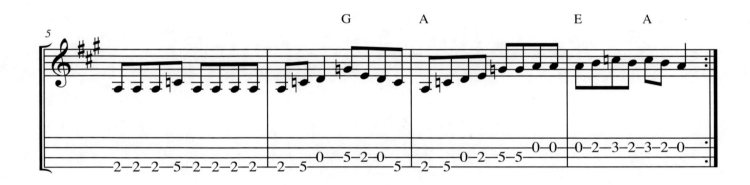

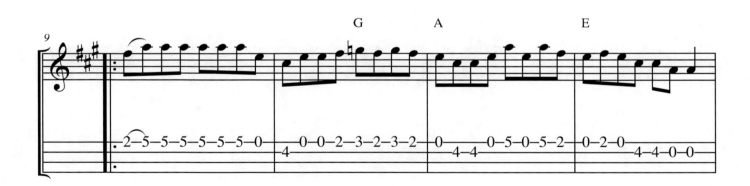

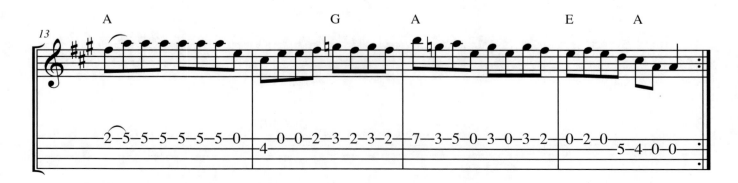

East Tennessee Blues - traditional

Source - Doc Watson and Bill Monroe - Off The Record, Vol. 2: Live Duet Recordings, 1963-1980 – Here is another tune where the C lick in measures 1-2 is moved over one set of strings in measures 3-4 for the lick in F. Play the double stop chords in measure 20 & 26 with the 1st and 3rd fingers.

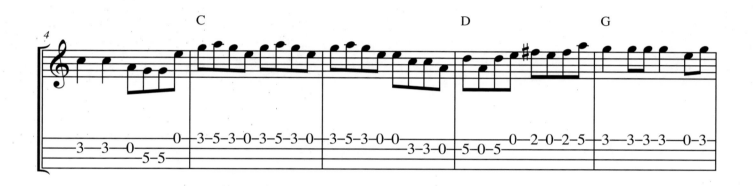

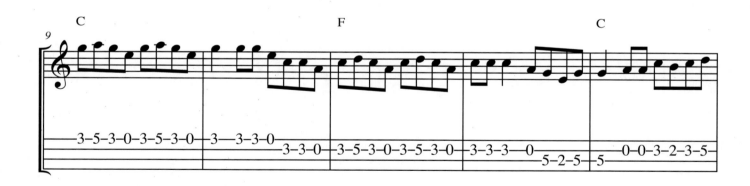

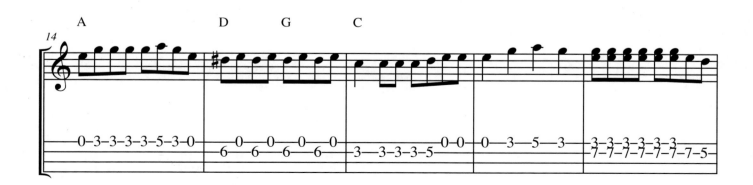

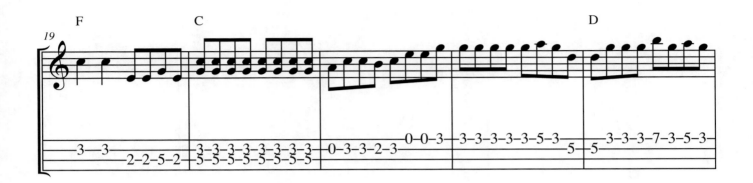
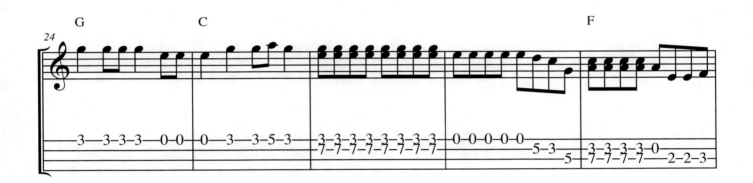
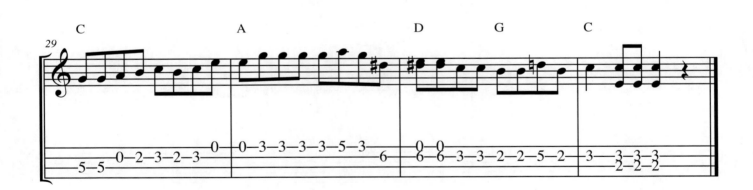

Monroe's Approach to Common Fiddle Tune Phrases

Below is a common nine note fiddle tune phrase in C. This phrase often occurs one measure before the end of a section. Monroe developed unique ways to simulate these phrases while reducing finger movement and therefore making the phrase easier to play quickly. Measures 1-2 require nine finger movements. Measures 3-4 require only three.

The G phrase below also requires nine movements. The phrase in measures 3-4 requires only three.

The D phrase below is like the G phrase above but moved over one string. This is an important concept to understand for developing mandolin players. (From *Soldier's Joy*.)

The A phrase is the most "notey" of the licks listed here. Nine moves in measures 1-2 and seven in 3-4.

Soldier's Joy - traditional

Source - The Music of Bill Monroe MCA Boxed Set - This solo was recorded with the B part first. It has been reversed here to the much more common AB form.

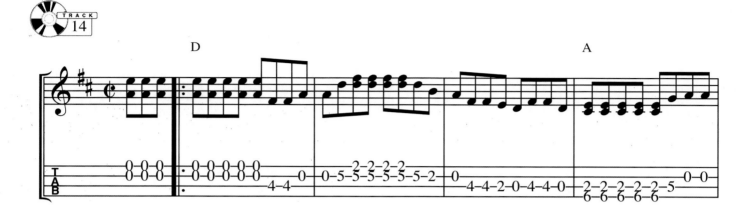

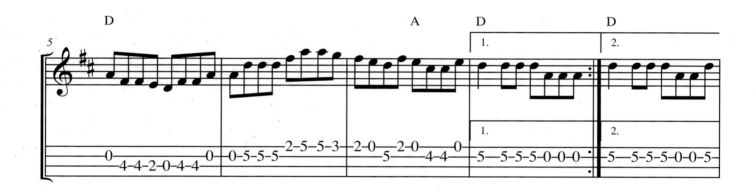

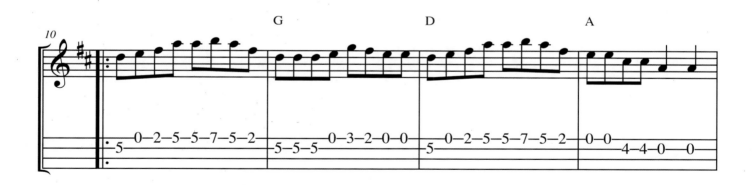

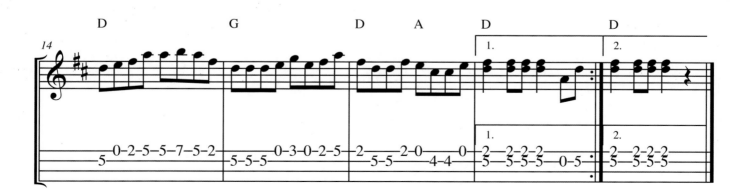

Arpeggios

Simply put, an arpeggio consists of the notes of a chord played one at a time rather than all together as a chord. As evidenced by his solos, Monroe was very familiar with arpeggios. Below are basic C, D. G and A major arpeggios followed by examples taken from the solos in this volume. Students are advised to spend time with these arpeggios until they can be played without hesitation. They are important building blocks for Monroe style solos. The C arpeggio below comes from *Back Up and Push*.

Some melodies consist primarily of arpeggio notes as in this example from *Turkey in the Straw*.

This example in the key of D comes from *Soldiers Joy*.

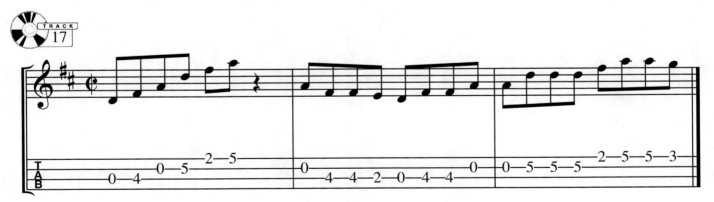

Here are two A arpeggio examples using both octaves of the 1st position A scale. The first example is from *Salt Creek* and uses the higher octave, Also in evidence is his use of doubled notes.

Here is the lower octave in an example taken from *Cotton Eyed Joe*.

Monroe used arpeggios in closed position solos extensively. Practice the closed arpeggio below until it is very familiar. This will make memorizing the following solos easier. This example is in the key of A. The chord numbers of the 15 notes in the two measures below are 1, 3, 5, 1, ♭3, 1, 5, 3, 1, ♭7, 5, 4, ♭3, 3, 1. This lick ends with a variation of a popular Monroe lick that detailed on page 51. Pay special attention to the fingering.

Chicken Reel - traditional

Source: Doc Watson and Bill Monroe - Off The Record, Vol. 2: Live Duet Recordings, 1963-1980 – This tune brings up the issue of left hand fingering. Normal mandolin fingering is 1st finger – frets 1 & 2; 2nd finger – frets 3 & 4; 3rd finger fret 5 & sometimes 6; 4th finger – frets 7 & sometimes 6. In measures 1, 2, 6, 8, 9, 10 & 12, the 1st finger plays both the first and second frets. In the B section, the third finger can shift up to the 7th fret in measure 19. The two open E string notes in that measure allow time for the shift up and back down.

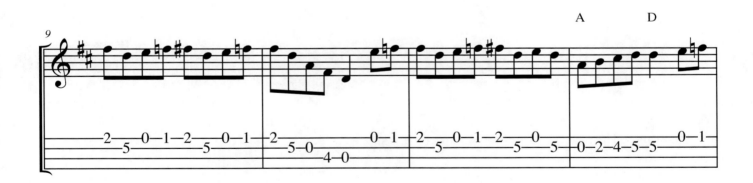

Katy Hill - traditional

Source: Bill Monroe - Off The Record, Vol. 1: Live Recordings, 1956-1969, Smithsonian Folkways– The G major pentatonic scale with a few additional notes serves as the note set for the A part of this fiddle tune. In the example below measures 1-2 shows a common "fiddle way" to play a phrase from *Katy Hill*. There are 9 eighth notes in the phrase requiring 9 left hand moves – a left hand move for every note. In measures 3-4 is a Monroe way of playing the same phrase using only 5 moves. By doubling the notes in the phrase and removing some of the scale tones, the left hand only plays 5 quarter notes while the right hand still picks all eighth notes. As a result, the left hand moves at half the speed of the right hand. This left hand efficiency helped Monroe play at rapid tempos. Practice playing measures 3-4 until they are effortless and smooth.

Recorded Sources

Listening to the original recordings is very important to capture the subtleties of Monroe's style. With a career that spanned many years and several recording formats, Monroe's music can be difficult to find. An effort was made in this volume to use recordings that are currently available through various popular internet sources. Here are some referenced recordings.

The Music of Bill Monroe MCA Boxed Set
Bill Monroe and the Bluegrass Boys: Off The Record, Vol. 1: Live Recordings, 1956-1969, Smithsonian Folkways
Bill Monroe and Doc Watson: Off The Record, Vol. 2: Live Duet Recordings, 1963-1980, Smithsonian Folkways
Kenny Baker Plays Bill Monroe - County
Bill Monroe CD B 1951-1954
Bill Monroe *16 Gems*

Katy Hill

This tune is similar to *Sally Johnson*.

Cripple Creek - traditional

Here is my simple arrangement of this classic fiddle tune in the Monroe style using characteristic Monroe approaches.

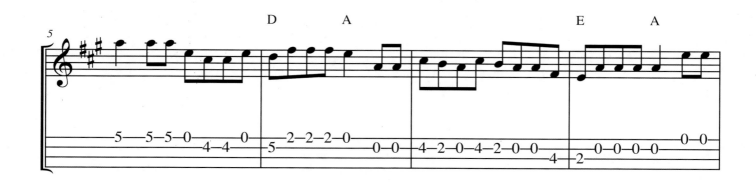

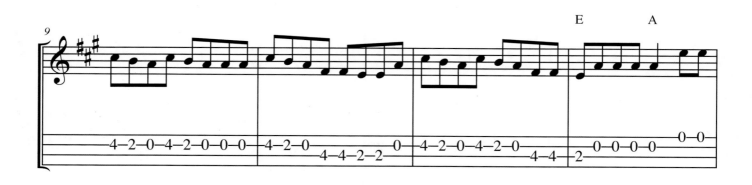

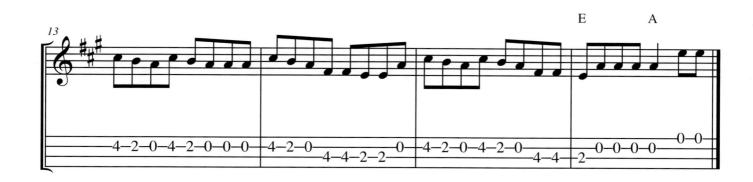

Fire On the Mountain - traditional

Source: Bill Monroe - Off The Record, Vol. 1: Live Recordings, 1956-1969, Smithsonian Folkways
– It is interesting that Monroe chooses to play G natural during the final E to A measure, as in measure 4, throughout the piece. Despite the presence of an E chord in the accompaniment which wants a G♯ note, Monroe signals by his note choice (G natural) that he hears a G chord at this place in the music.

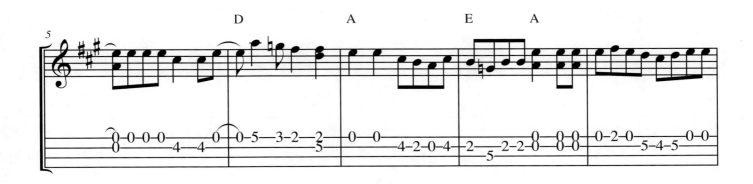

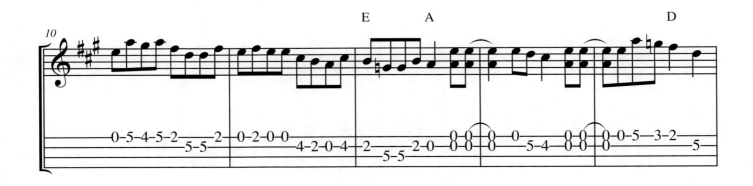

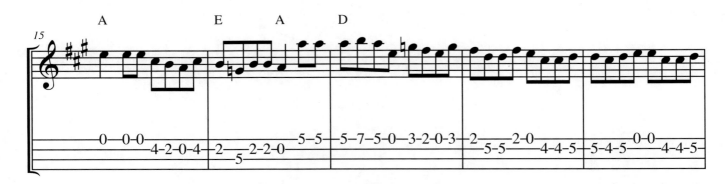

Gospel Turnarounds I

In bluegrass music, full-length solos are seldom played in gospel songs. Typically, a shorter four-measure *turnaround* is played to introduce the song and to separate verses. These turnarounds often do not contain any melody of the song so they can be used in and are interchangeable with many songs. The mandolin is a popular lead instrument on these turnarounds often accompanied only by rhythm guitar. Here are two Monroe turnarounds in the keys of A and G. The tie in measure 3 of the 2nd turnaround indicates 2 consecutive pull-offs,

The first turnaround comes from *Happy on My Way* (The Music of Bill Monroe MCA Boxed Set.) A full solo of this song appears later in this volume. The second turnaround comes from *The Old Crossroads* (Bill Monroe *16 Gems*.)

Paddy on the Turnpike - traditional

Source - Doc Watson and Bill Monroe - Off The Record, Vol. 2: Live Duet Recordings, 1963-1980, Smithsonian Folkways - A similar movement saving G lick as described in the notes to *Katy Hill* appears throughout this transcription in measures 5, 13, 17, 21 and 29.

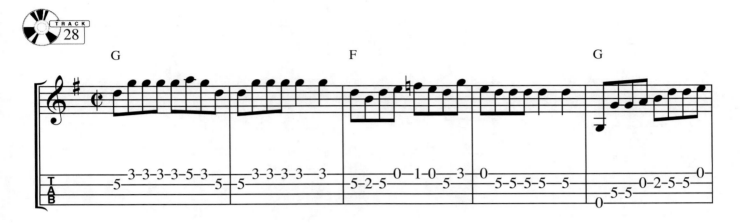

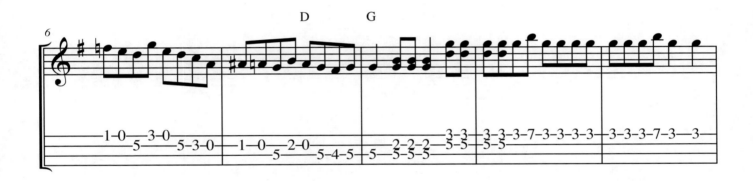

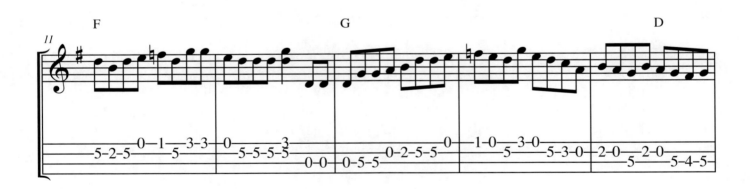

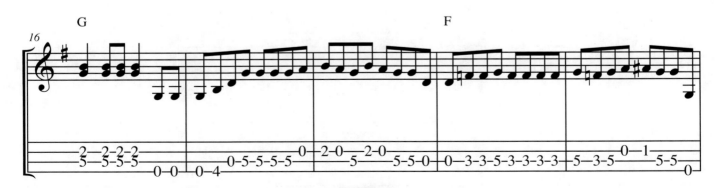

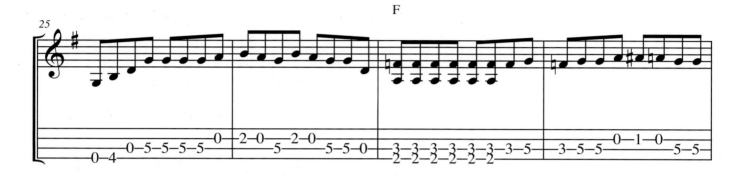

Gospel Turnarounds II - A Voice From On High

Source: The Music of Bill Monroe MCA Boxed Set - This song was recorded in non-standard tuning. A little detective work may explain this. Monroe is quoted as saying about this song: "I wrote the chorus to that song and I meant for the tenor to have the high part there, and it was about high as I could sing." To achieve the highest key he could sing, Monroe may have tuned the mandolin to suit his voice. The result was E♭, which Monroe likely would have preferred to play in E position. By tuning the entire band down roughly a half step, he achieved the key he wanted in a familiar position.

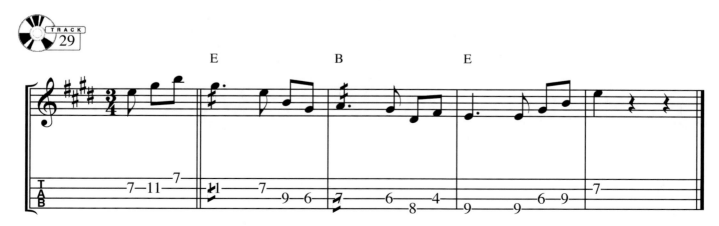

Sally Goodin - traditional

Source - The Music of Bill Monroe MCA Boxed Set – It is interesting that despite the accompaniment being in A major, Monroe plays the A part using the minor or blusey sounding C natural rather than C♯. He then plays the B part in the major key.

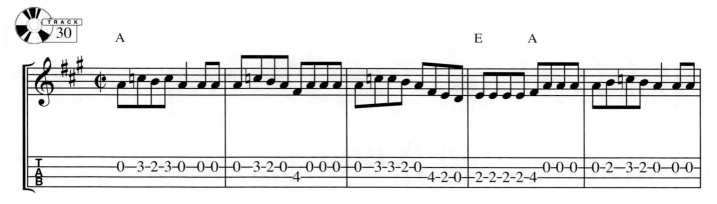

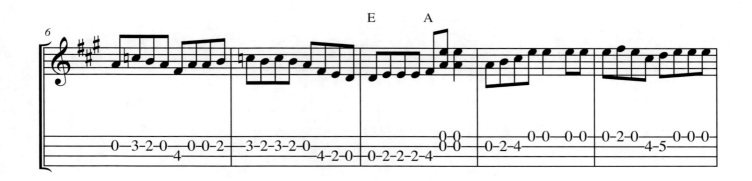

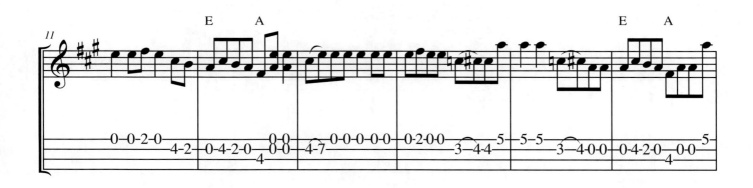

Panhandle Country - Bill Monroe

Source: This is another great signature instrumental. The descending line in measures 5-6 over the G chord makes good use of open strings to produce a lick playable at high speed.

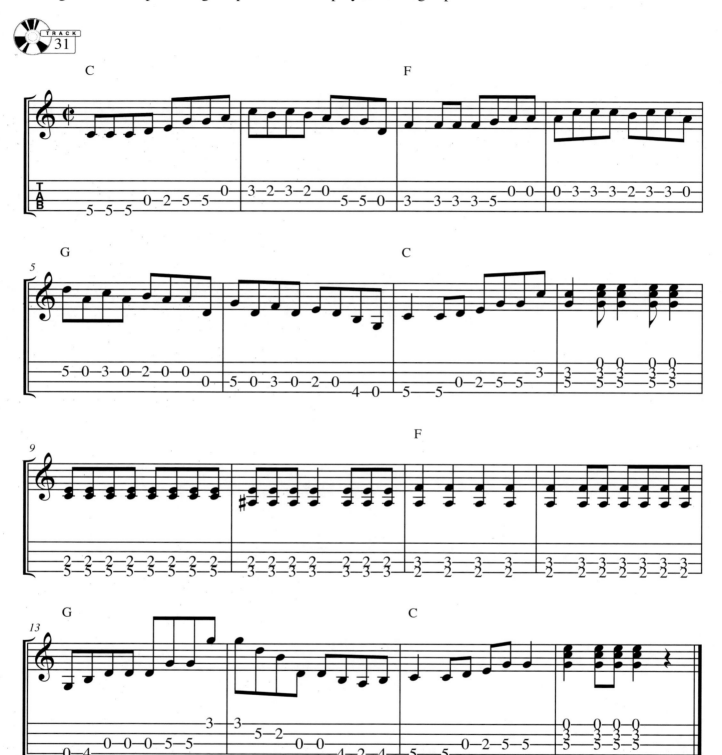

Back Up and Push - traditional

Source - The Music of Bill Monroe MCA Boxed Set – Recorded in 1941, this solo bears remarkable resemblance to measures 9-16 of *Rawhide* – Monroe's 1951 tour de force. Moving to second position in measure 1 (first finger at the third fret,) allows the F lick to be played easily and quickly.

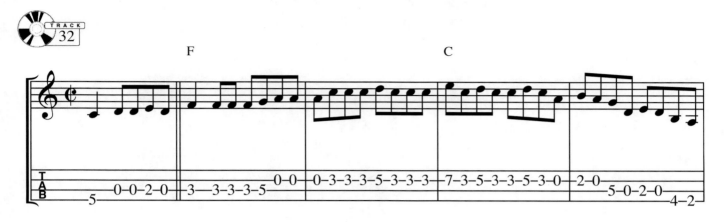

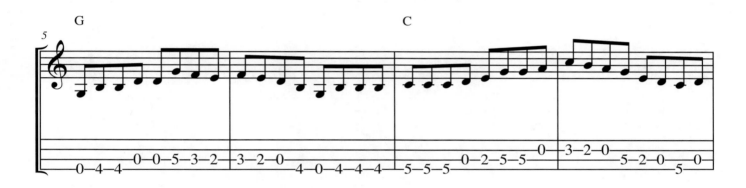

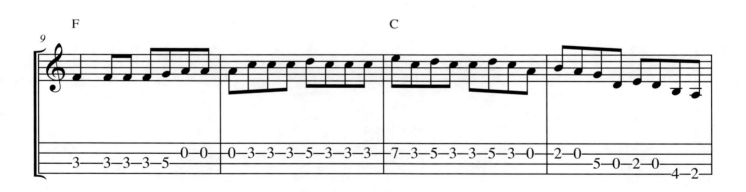

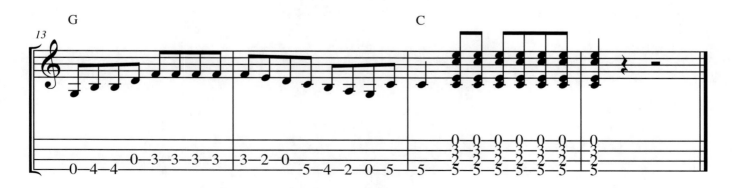

Roanoke - Bill Monroe

Source - The Music of Bill Monroe MCA Boxed Set – Here is another of Monroe's signature instrumentals. On his recordings of the tune, he only plays the A section leaving the B section for the fiddles. The first staff is the introduction which Monroe plays solo before the fiddles start the tune. The pick up notes in measure 4 are played only if the mandolin takes the first solo. Note the doubled notes throughout that slow the left hand. The 7th fret in measure 8 is played with the 4th finger.

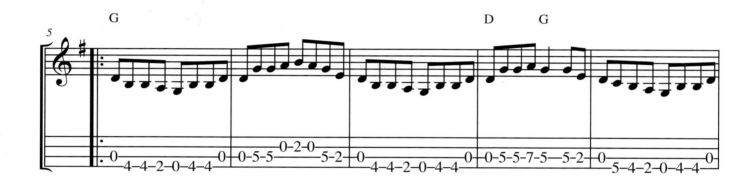

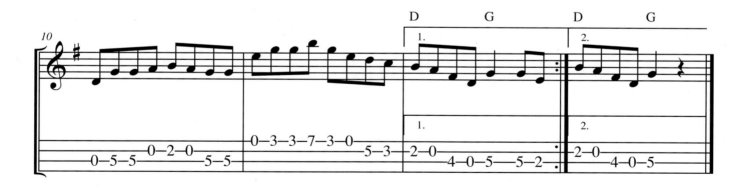

Turkey in the Straw - traditional

 Source: Doc Watson and Bill Monroe - Off The Record, Vol. 2: Live Duet Recordings, 1963-1980, Smithsonian Folkways – This is played very quickly. Monroe makes great use of his characteristic repeating note figures throughout. To perform this well, it should be memorized. Monroe created these kinds of solos at tempo and the flow and sense of music really vanishes at slower speeds. The G major arpeggio occurs throughout.

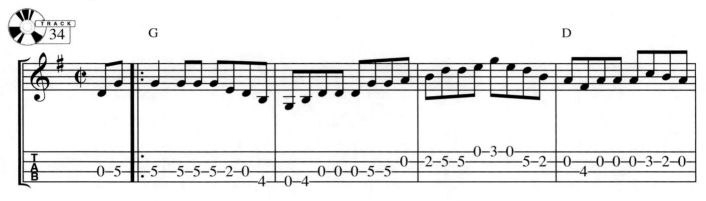

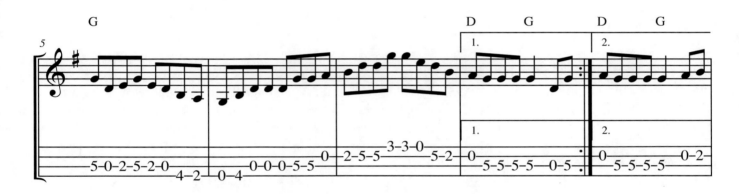

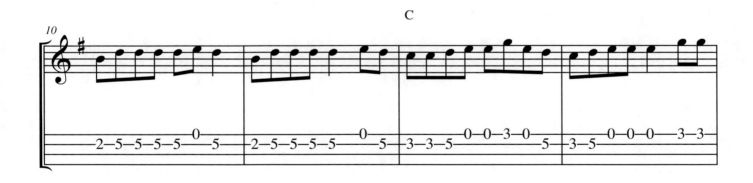

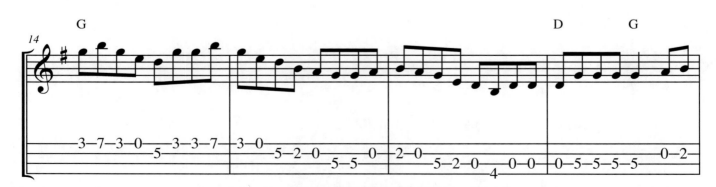

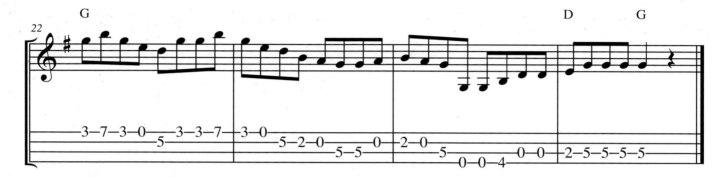

Monroe's Closed Position Solos

All the fiddle tune solos in the 1st section of this volume have been in open keys played in open position. These were in the fiddle/mandolin friendly keys of C, G. D and A. When Monroe sang however, he often chose keys such as B♭, B or C that suited his tenor voice. With no clear model to guide him, he invented a unique approach and a lick vocabulary to allow him to solo and improvise in these challenging keys. For many fans, it is the sound of these solo breaks played with Monroe's unique attack and sense of rhythm that defines the Monroe mandolin style.

The approach is not a melodic one. While his fiddle tune playing generally stayed close to the accepted melody, his song solos typically did not. Solos were assembled from a set of pre-learned licks that could be lined up in a way to fit the chord progression of a given song. The solo therefore, would fit the chord changes of the song, but might not even hint at the melody of that given song.

In the cases of *On and On, Never Again (Will I knock Upon Your Door,) Out in the Cold World* and *I'll Never Shed Another Tear,* we have four songs that share the same chord progression. It is:

```
1 1 4 1
1 1 5 5
1 1 4 1
1 5 1 1
```

or for example:

```
G G C G    A A D A    B B E B
G G D D    A A E E    B B F♯ F♯
G G C G    A A D A    B B E B
G D G G    A E A A    B F♯ B B
```

Monroe's solo to each of these songs as a result might be similar.

The Gold Rush - Bill Monroe

Source: – This instrumental is one of the most popular of all Monroe tunes. It is played at nearly every bluegrass jam session. The version played here is taken from a live performance in Monroe's last decade of life. It shows how Monroe's power as a mandolin player stayed present throughout his career. A few notes have been changed to reflect the generally accepted melody.

Alan Munde, Bill Monroe, Jimmy Martin, Berryville, Virginia, 1969.

Bill Monroe, Mike Seeger, Mother Maybelle Carter, Berryville, Virginia, 1969.

Vic Jordan, Kenny Baker, Monroe, Roland White, Doug (AKA Ranger Doug) Green. Sunset Park, West Grove, Pennsylvania, 1968. Note the peeking boy between Baker and Monroe.

Former Bluegrass Boys Bill "Brad" Keith (banjo) and Peter Rowan (guitar) join Monroe on stage. Berkshire Mountain Festival, Possibly 1976.

Monroe, Rual Yarborough, Chubby Wise, Clyde Moody. Bill Yates, Berryville, Virginia, 1969

Kenny Baker and Monroe, New York Law School, Possibly 1973.

Kenny Baker, Tex Logan, Monroe, Red Smiley, Berryville, Virginia, 1969.

Monroe and Steve Arkin, New York Law School. Possibly 1973.

Monroe and Curtis Blackwell, Berryville, Virginia, 1969

Kenny Baker, Rual Yarborough, Monroe, Fred Bortenstein, Mac Wiseman, James Monroe, Berryville, Virginia, 1969

Bessie Lee Mauldin, Bobby Hicks, Vassar Clements, Monroe, Charlie Cline, New River Ranch,
Maryland, 1955.

Jack Hicks, Tex Logan, Monroe, Jim Rooney, Bill Box, (possibly) McBurney YMCA.
Date unknown.

Ted Lundy, Monroe and Dan Lundy, New York Law School, Possibly 1973.

Jack Hicks, Monroe, Wayne Lewis and Joe Stuart.
Note missing "Gibson" inlay in mandolin headstock. Delaware. Possibly 1973.

Kenny Baker, Bob Black, Monroe, Randy Davis, Berkshire Mountain Festival. Possibly 1976.

Jim Moratto, Monroe, Greg Kennedy (partially obscured,) 1974. Location unknown.

Charlie Cline (mandolin,) Bill and Charlie Monroe at the New River Ranch
Country Music Park, Rising Sun, Maryland., 1955.

Monroe without his trademark Gibson. Unknown location and date.

Monroe and Don Reno, Berryville, Virginia, 1969

Long time Bluegrass Boy Kenny Baker and Monroe, Wilmington, Delaware, date unknown.

The classic Monroe stance. Delaware, date uknown.

Kenny Baker, Monroe and Bill Box. Monroe is playing another different mandolin.
Delaware, Possibly 1973.

Bill Monroe and Wayne Lewis. Note the missing scroll on the mandolin headstock.
Berkshire Mountain Festival, late 1970s.

Chubby Wise, Rual Yarborough and Monroe, Berryville, Virginia, 1969

Monroe and Clyde Moody, Berryville, Virginia, 1969

Monroe and Red Smiley, Berryville, Virginia, 1969

Former Bluegrass Boy Byron Berline and Monroe, Philadelphia Folk Festival, date unknown.

A big finale. Tex Logan (fiddle,) Ted Lundy (banjo,) Ben Pedigo (banjo,)
Monroe and Dan Paisley (guitar,) New York Law School, Possibly 1973.

Curley Ray Cline, Bill Monroe, Ralph Stanley, Larry Sparks A forest of microphones!
Berryville, Virginia, 1969

Monroe and Joe Stuart backstage, Philadelphia Folk Festival, ca. 1971-73.

Jack Hicks, Monroe and Joe Stuart. Wilmington, Delaware. Date unknown. Note Monroe's model left hand form - four fingers down, wrist away from the neck.

Bill and son, James Monroe, McBurney YMCA, date unknown.

Monroe Blues - Joe Carr

Bill Monroe recorded many 12 bar blues songs including *Muleskinner Blues, Brakeman Blues, White House Blues, Heavy Traffic Ahead, Rocky Road Blues* and several of Jimmy Rodger's numbered *Blue Yodels*. His approach to these songs was very hard driving and bluesy - something that had never been heard on the mandolin before. He played many of these songs in the chop position - a position in which he developed several signature licks. In the "chop" keys of G, A, B♭, B and even C, he played a blistering downstroke driven style that would have sounded right at home on the guitar in the hands of early rock and rollers like Chuck Berry.

Below is a blues written by the author that contains many of Monroe's favorite blues licks including perhaps the most elusive - the ending lick played in measures 7 and 12.

The solo starts with a two note chord in the chop position using fingers 2 and 3. In measure 2, the little finger reaches up to frets 8 and 9 for a bluesy sound. The rest of the first staff stays in the chop position including the slide from 3 to 4 in measure 3 with the 1st finger. The first finger shifts to the 5th fret for measure 4 and shifts back to chop position in measure 6. The lick in measure 7 deserves special attention. The triplet covering frets 9, 8 and 7 is played with a quick DUD "flick" of the pick. While this flick is happening, the left hand 4th finger is descending over the 9th, 8th and 7th frets in coordination with the pick strokes. This demanding lick takes much pracrice to master. The lick appears in several easier variations shown on the next page.

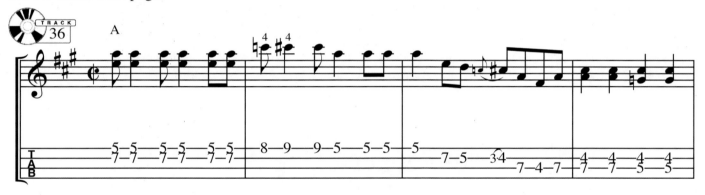

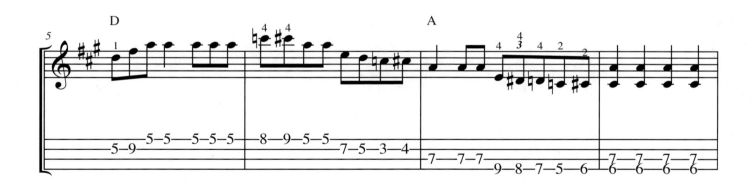

Monroe Blues Shapes and Licks

The chop position generates several bluesy sounds within the basic shape of the chord. Here are 6 double stops that can be considered part of the shape. Measure 1 is the 3 and 1 note of the basic chord. Measure 2 adds the 3rd finger to get the 5 and 1 notes of the chord. Measures 3 is the minor 3rd and 5th. Measure 4 is the 1 and 3 of the chord while measure 5 is the flat 7 and 3. The final measure is not in the normal chop shape, but is the 3 and 1 of the chord.

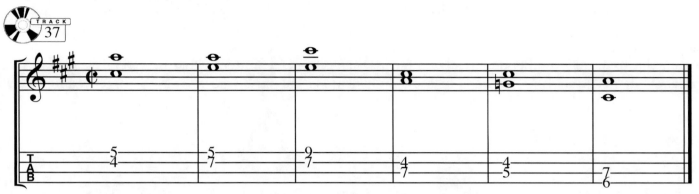

The licks below are all considered "in the shape." If you visualize these licks in this manner, you will be able to move them easily to other "chop" keys. The first 5 licks are all similar and appear throughout this volume. They can be interchanged as you develop your own solos. The licks in measures 6-11 are variations of the ending lick detailed previously in the *Monroe Blues*.

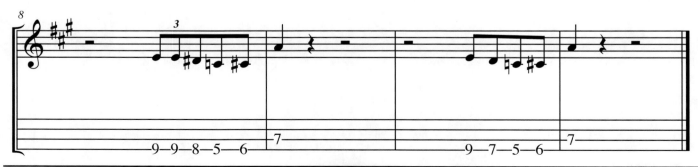

White House Blues

Source: Bill Monroe and the Bluegrass Boys: Off The Record, Vol. 1: Live Recordings, 1956-1969, Smithsonian Folkways – This live solo in B features several classic moves. The recurring open A note in measure 3 is the flat 7 note of the B chord which may sound jarring at slow speeds but provides a good continuous flow of eighth notes at full speed. This motif is continued with the open repeated D ($\flat$3) string in measures 2 and 4. The lick in measure 11 is a simplified version (without the triplet) of the Monroe lick introduced in *Monroe Blues*. Once you have memorized this solo, play it one fret lower in B$\flat$ and one fret higher in C. You'll find that although the open strings may become even more jarring in these keys, they serve the purpose of keeping the uninterrupted flow of eighth notes. With practice, you'll learn to de-emphasize these less important (and non-musical) notes for better effect. Monroe used this technique to great effect on fast solos. This technique is one of his unique and most controversial soloing inventions.

White House Blues II

Source: The Music of Bill Monroe MCA Boxed Set – This tune was a showcase for Monroe and his banjo picker Rudy Lyle. On the 1954 studio recording Monroe takes four (!) blistering solos. The first and fourth solos are similar to the live recording solo on the opposite page. This is his second solo from the studio recording in which he uses the power of the closed B "chop" position. The minor third blues lick in measures 3 and 4 gives a powerful, almost rock and roll type, sound to the solo.

Using the chop position, measures 0-4 are played with the 2nd and 3rd fingers. Shift in measure 5 and play the first notes with the 1st finger.keeping this position through measure 6. Return to the chop position in measures 7 and 8 using the 4th finger for both the 10th and 11th frets in measure 7. For the F♯ chord use finger 2 for both the 7th and 8th frets and continue with this fingering through measure10. Return to the chop position in measure 11 and play that measure with fingers 4, and 2 finishing in measure 12 with the 3rd finger.

White House Blues III

Source:The Music of Bill Monroe MCA Boxed Set – Here is solo three from the studio recording. Monroe plays a single note eighth note "tremolo" of sorts. Again we are in the chop position in measures 0-4. The little finger plays both frets 10 and 11 in measure 1. Shift to the 1st finger again in measure 5 returning to the chop position in measures 7 and 8. Finger measures 9-12 as in version II.

Notice the flat 7 note in measure 4 that signals the chord change to E. The ending lick in measures 11 and 12 is a variation of the one in version II.

Bb Chop Position Solo - Joe Carr

This solo fits the chord changes on page 32. In measure 3, move over a set of strings and play the Eb chord at frets 8, 5 and 6 of the 4th, 3rd and 2nd strings. To get the Monroe sound, this solo should be played with all downstrokes.

Roll On Buddy, Roll On - Teddy Wilburn, Doyle Wilburn

Source: Bill Monroe - Off The Record, Vol. 1: Live Recordings, 1956-1969, Smithsonian Folkways – This solo begins with the B "chop" position. The repeated lick in measures 8-10 shows how effective a simple musical idea can be. The A note at the 5th fret in measure 11 is the flat 7 of the B chord, giving a very bluesy sound to the solo.

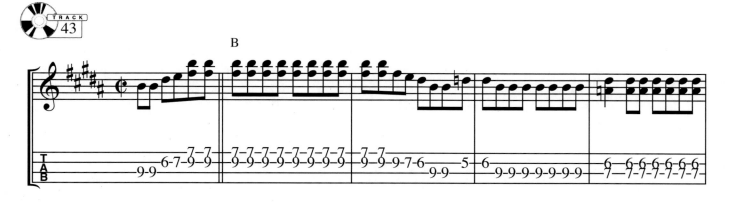

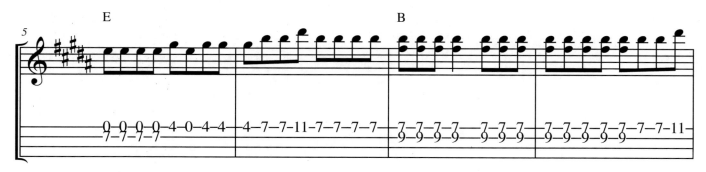

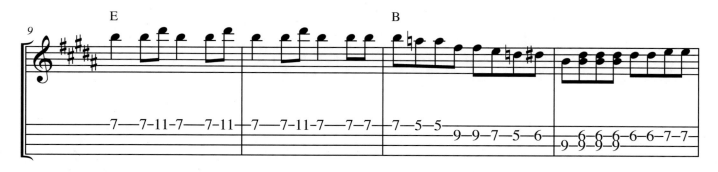

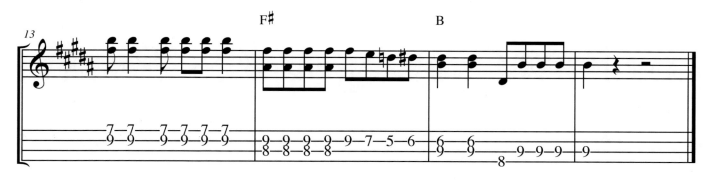

Wheel Hoss - Bill Monroe

Source: Bill Monroe - Off The Record, Vol. 1: Live Recordings, 1956-1969, Smithsonian Folkways -
Here is a major Monroe style instrumental and an example of how he took liberties. Here he plays only 12
measures of the A part instead of the expected 16 as played by the fiddles. The small square in measure 21
indicates these notes are to be played as harmonics at the 12th fret. A light touch by the side of the 3rd or 4th
finger directly over the fret while picking the string will produce the desired effect.

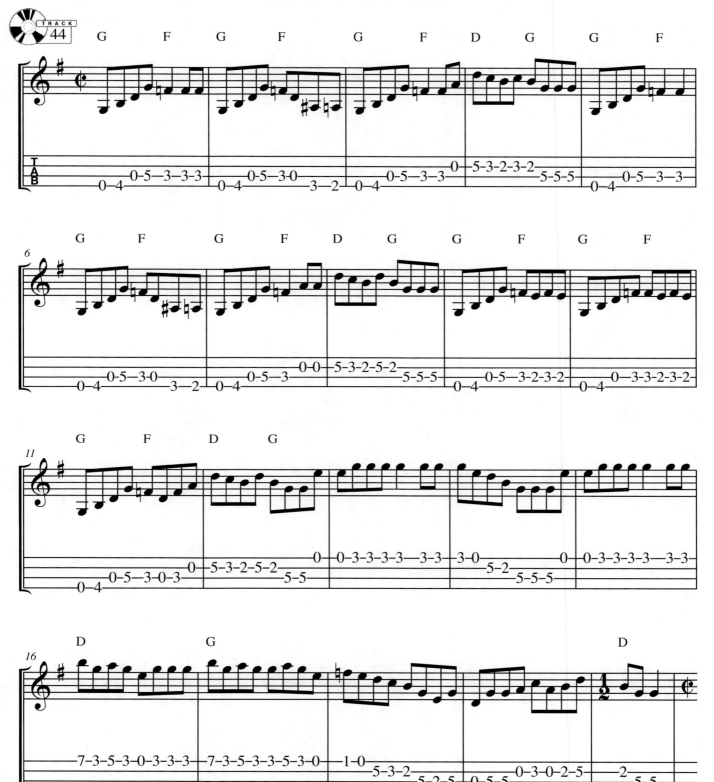

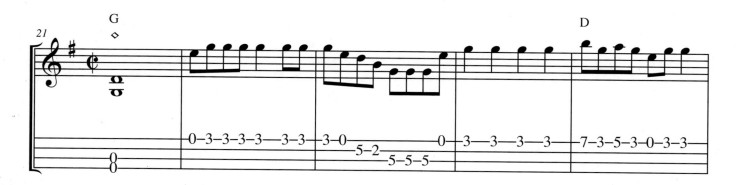

Gospel Turnarounds III

This is an A turnaround from *Angels Rock Me to Sleep*.

This is a G turnaround from *Lord Protect My Soul*.

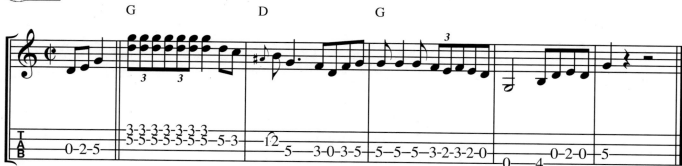

Roll In My Sweet Baby's Arms - traditional

Source: Bill Monroe - Off The Record, Vol. 1: Live Recordings, 1956-1969, Smithsonian Folkways - Here is a bluegrass standard perhaps most associated with Flatt and Scruggs but performed live here by Monroe with singer Hazel Dickens. Playing in open position, Monroe chooses some unusual notes such as the flat 3 (1st fret) in measure 3.

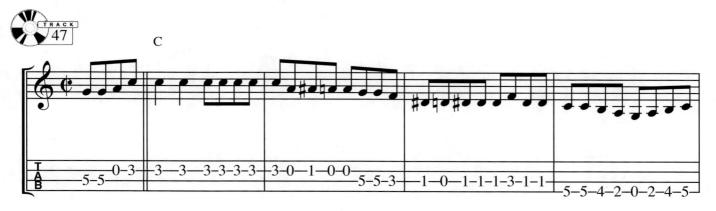

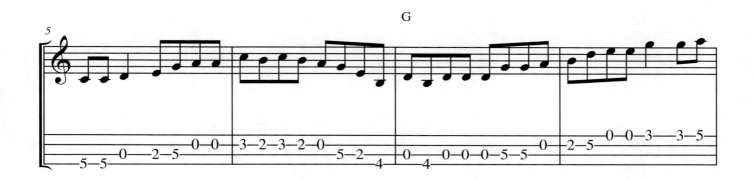

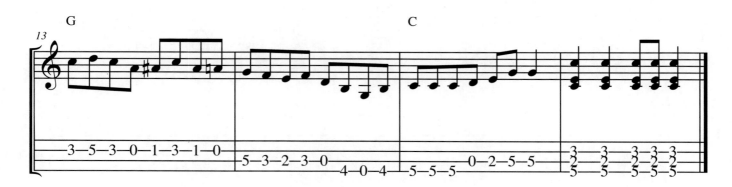

Kentucky Mandolin - Bill Monroe

Source: The Music of Bill Monroe MCA Boxed Set - Here is a major Monroe style instrumental in G minor. Minor keys are unusual in bluegrass making this tune even more unique.

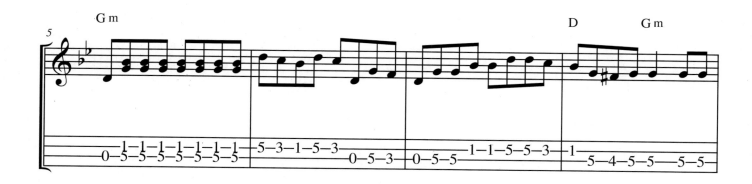

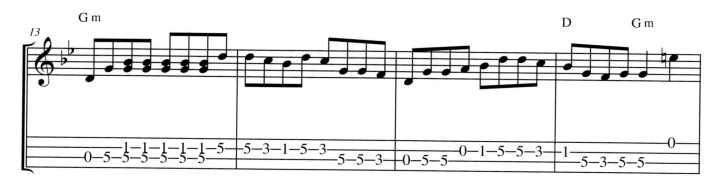

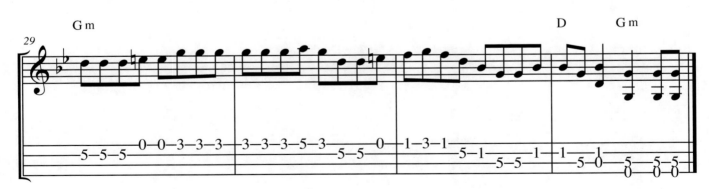

Methodist Preacher - traditional

Source: The Music of Bill Monroe MCA Boxed Set - Here is my take on how Monroe would play this old time favorite. Kenny Baker fiddles it on "Uncle Pen" with Monroe on rhythm.

Nine Pound Hammer

Source: The Music of Bill Monroe MCA Boxed Set - Here is Monroe at his most aggressive and perhaps, playful. For most of the solo, he plays very stacatto chord chops that only outline the chord progression and not the melody. Aim the pick in measures 3-4 outward so that the A string doesn't sound when the G and D strings are played. Release tension after each chord is played so the sound is cut off, making each chord stroke sound separate.

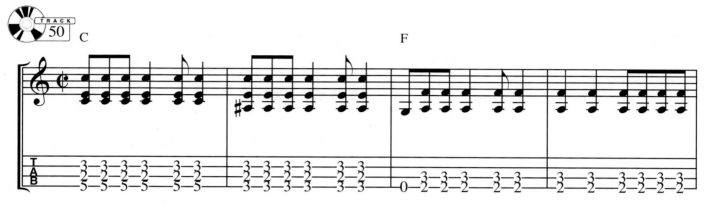

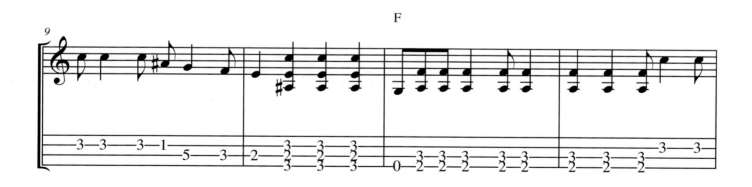

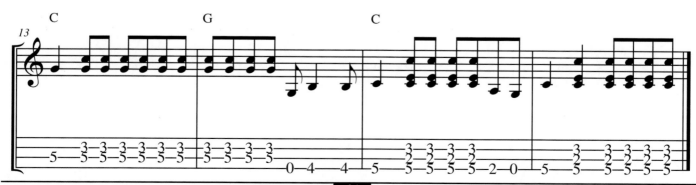

Walk Softly on this Heart - Bill Monroe

Source: The Music of Bill Monroe MCA Boxed Set - This is a great example of how Monroe used the "chop" position and tremolo to produce a melody based solo. For ease of reading, the melody notes have been written as eighth notes. They are actually played as tremolo and are more like three notes per beat than the two per beat that is written. Notice how the flat seven note (G) in measure 8, sets up the move to the D chord in measure 9.

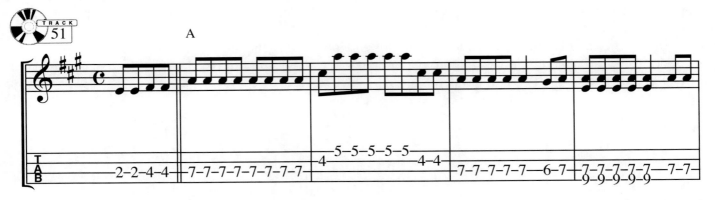

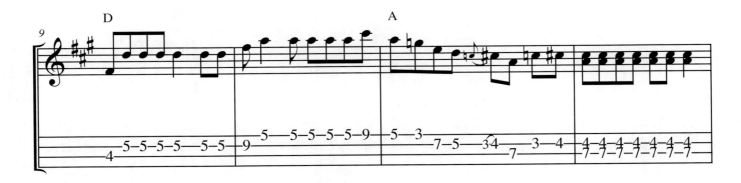

Blackberry Blossom - traditional

Bill Monroe never recorded this popular fiddle tune. I borrowed 2 techniques Monroe used extensively, note repetition and efficient solo design to create a solo he might have played had he ever recorded it. As previously mentioned, to keep an uninterrupted flow of eighth notes, Monroe would often repeat a note rather than play a series or run of notes as a fiddler might. The resulting phrase gives the impression of a continuous musical flow while using fewer left hand moves. The resulting phrase is therefore easier to play rapidly.

Monroe re-stated certain musical phrases to make them more playable on the mandolin. This designed-for-speed approach allowed him to play tunes much more quickly.

Blackberry Blossom features a complex eighth note melody that is challenging at high speed. By varying the melody, repeating certain notes and removing others, I've devised a solo that retains the general shape of the original melody while becoming much more playable.

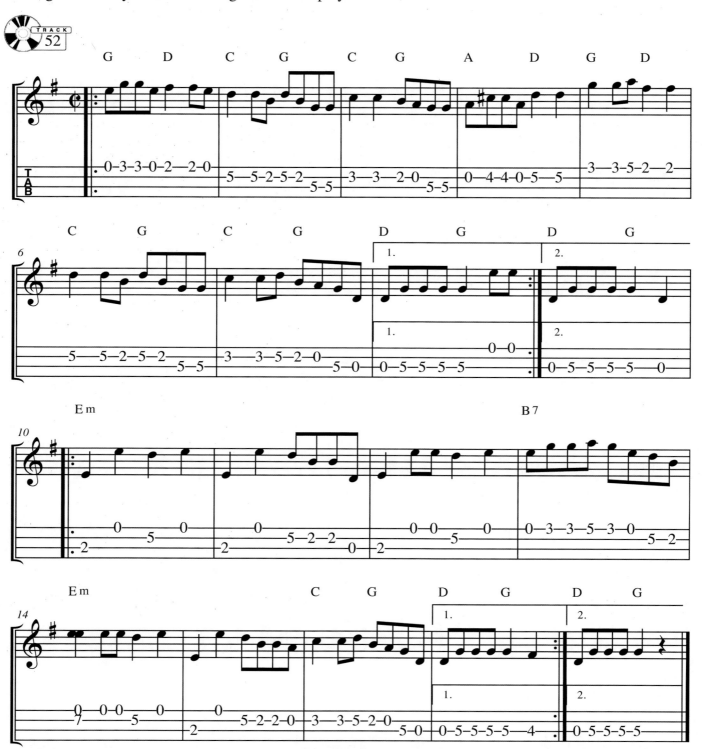

Tremolo

Tremolo, the rapid down up down up movement of the pick, is a popular technique among mandolin players to extend notes beyond an eighth note length. It is used extensively in the classical and Italian styles. The tremolo in these styles is typically very fast and may be based on 32nd or 64th notes. Monroe tended to play a slower tremolo based on eighth note triplets or sixteenth notes. He used this technique primarily on slower vocal songs and the duration of the note might be from a quarter note to perhaps 2 whole notes in length. See examples on *Close By, The First Whippoorwill* and others.

Tremolo is especially effective on two note chords. The examples below show a G chord in both the eighth note triplet based and 16th note tremolo.

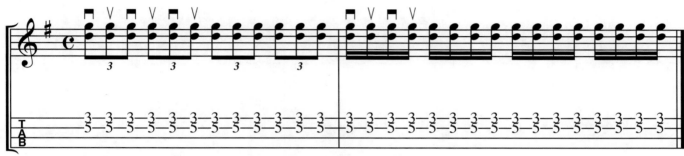

Special Tunings

No work on Monroe's style would be complete without attention to his special mandolin tunings. The idea of tuning the individual strings of the mandolin to different pitches appears to be another Monroe invention. The idea was likely inspired by fiddlers who re-tuned their 4 string instruments for specific tunes. The most famous tune with this effect is *Get Up John* (1953) although special tunings were also used on *Bluegrass Ramble* (1950,) *Memories of You (1950,)* the evocative *My Last Days on Earth* (1981) and others.

The *Get Up John* tuning is the most popular. Mandolin players Buzz Busby and Dean Webb of the Dillards both wrote original instrumentals using this tuning. Most recently, Ricky Skaggs has made *Get Up John* a *tour de force* in his stage show. Here are instructions for the tuning. The outside E string is lowered to D, in unison with the 5th fret, A (2nd) string. The other E is tuned down a 5th to match the open 2nd (A) strings. The 2nd and 3rd strings remain tuned to A and D respectively.

The outside G (4th) string is tuned up a whole step to A, one octave below the A string. The inside G string is tuned down a half step to F#, one octave below the F# at the 4th fret of the D string. Once these adjustments have been made, every string will need to be re-tuned to pitch. If tuned well, an open strum of all strings will produce a pleasant D chord.

The process of re-tuning is so time intensive that Monroe kept a second mandolin in this tuning. This may explain the different mandolins seen in the photo section. Rhythm is limited with only two note chords available on the untouched A and D strimgs.

The tuning for *My Last Days on Earth* is an F tuning that spells A, A (4,) D, D (3,) A, C (2,) and D, F (1) from low to high. It is available at www.mandozine.com as a tefview download. Monroe never used this tuning for another song.

Brakeman's Blues

Source: Bill Monroe and the Bluegrass Boys: Off The Record, Vol. 1: Live Recordings, 1956-1969, Smithsonian Folkways - This live solo was played with Monroe's insistant all-down picking. Open strings in measures 6, 8 and 9 keep the flow of eighth notes. Note the slow first finger slide in measures 3 to 4. This slide is played much more slowly that the grace note slides in measure 7. Also note the triplet chord in measure 6 (requiring an upstroke) and the slide in measure 8. In measure 12, there is another version of the closed position ending lick introduced in *Monroe's Blues*. Here it is played without the triplet and the last note in the measure is played twice. The lesson here is that there are several "less perfect" ways to play this lick that still retains the same musical "feel" at performance tempo.

No One But My Darlin' - Bill Monroe

Source: Bluegrass 1950-58 Bill Monroe

Here is a simple 2 chord song with lots of great features. The opening 2 measures uses a sweeping G major arpeggio covering all 4 strings. Measure 3 uses the triplet figure. The lick in measure 5 is repeated in measures 9 and 13.

I Saw the Light - Hank Williams

Source: Bill Monroe CD:B 1951-1954 - Here is a solo to a great standard written by singer Hank Williams. This is so well known that it is hard to realize it was a relatively new song when Monroe recorded it in 1957. This version in B begin and ends with the signature Monroe lick detailed earlier. Most of this solo can be used to create solos for songs in B♭, B, C and even high D.

Happy on My Way - Pete Pyle

Source: Bill Monroe CD:B 1951-1954 - Here is an unusual recording of a gospel song. There is the expected turnaround after the 1st verse followed by two complete solos later in the song. This is the second solo. Be careful not to get lost in the repeating lick in measures 9-11.

Close By

Source: The Music of Bill Monroe MCA Boxed Set: - Here is another great one. It is a good example of Monroe's slow tremolo. The solo is in the chop position. Use the 4th finger for the 8-9 move in measure 2. The A7 in measure 4 sets up the move to D. The ending lick in measure 15 is another variation of this Monroe staple.

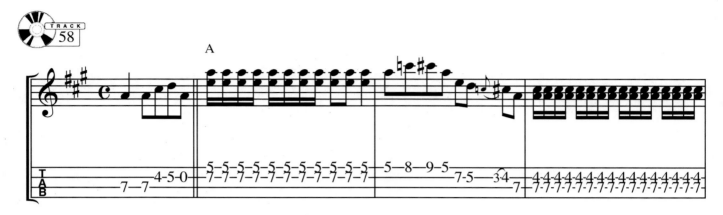

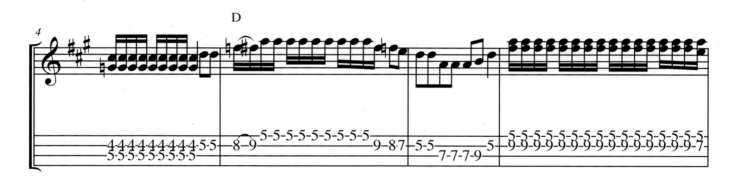

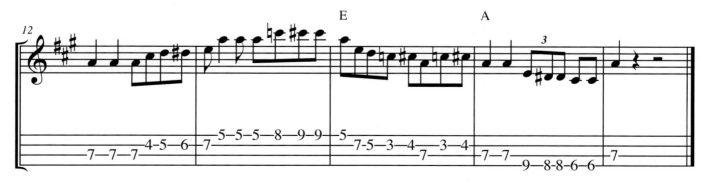

Fast Song in G

  Here is a solo that fits this progression: 1144 1155 1144 1511. It is played very fast and is great example of Monroe powerfully "going for it." He uses an entire measure as a pickup to establish the speed. Measures 2-5 seem at first to be an improvised phrase that moves from G to C. This phase is repeated, however, almost identically in measures 10-13, implying this is a rehearsed phrase. Measures 1, 6 and 10 share the same sweeping G lick. Notice the similarlities to the G lick (measure 14) and the D lick (measure 15.) The entire solo is designed for speed and was likely improvised (from pre-learned parts) in real time.

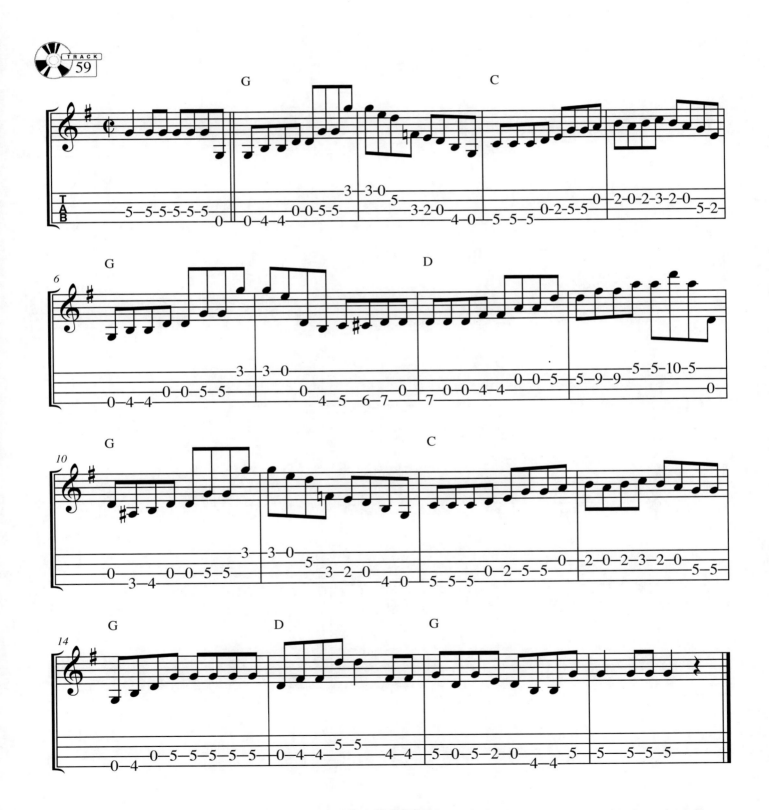

Little Joe

Source: The Music of Bill Monroe MCA Boxed Set - Here is a great solo in D for this sentimental favorite. We have D7 chords in measures 2 and 6 setting up the move to G. Throughout we have the power of unison A and D notes using the open strings. The open G and D strings at the end of measures 2 and 10 are examples of anticipation. The D major arpeggio appears in measure 15.

Sugar Coated Love - Audrey Butler

Source: The Music of Bill Monroe MCA Boxed Set - This 1951 duet with Monroe and lead singer Carter Stanley is in the key of C. The ragtime lick is effective in measures 3 and 16.

The First Whippoorwill - Bill Monroe

Source: The Music of Bill Monroe MCA Boxed Set - Here is a great introduction in G for this 1951 duet between Monroe and guitarist Edd Mayfield. The recording appears to be in G$\sharp$ although the mandolin is clearly played in open G position. Bluegrass bands of this period often recorded with their instruments tuned above standard pitch. This was likely to get a brighter sound from the instruments or, as I suspect in this case, to better suit the singers voices.

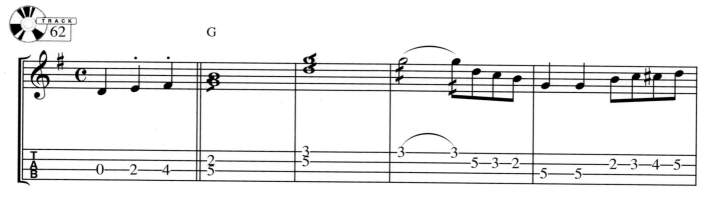

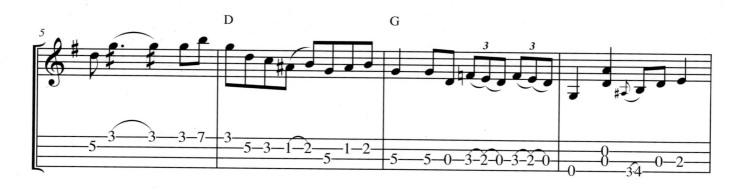

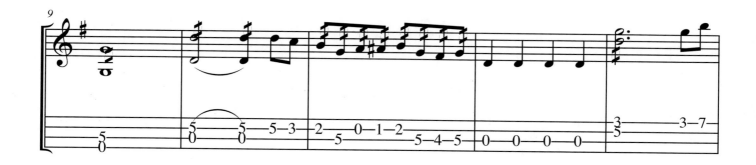

Can't You Hear Me Callin' - Bill Monroe

Source: The Music of Bill Monroe MCA Boxed Set - The two dots in the pickup masure indicate short notes. Be sure to use slow tremolo throughout.

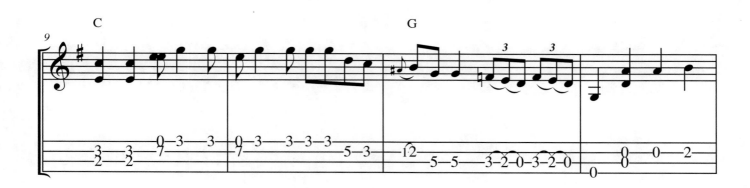

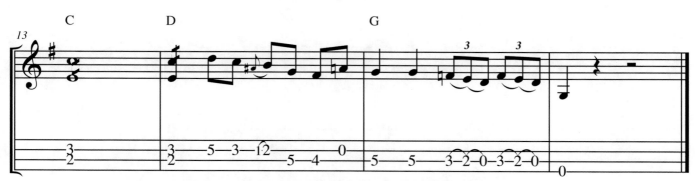

I'm On My Way Back to the Old Home - Bill Monroe

Source: The Music of Bill Monroe MCA Boxed Set. Here is another song recorded with the instruments tuned 1/2 step sharp. This may have been to make the instruments sound brighter, to better suit the vocal or in a day before electronic tuners, the band may have just tuned their instruments to Monroe's mandolin, which may have been sharp. This A solo is full of easy and effective licks. Consider the D licks and the one in measure 14.

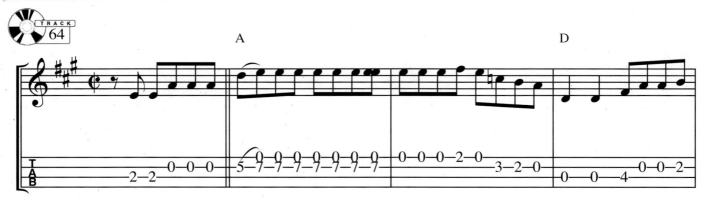

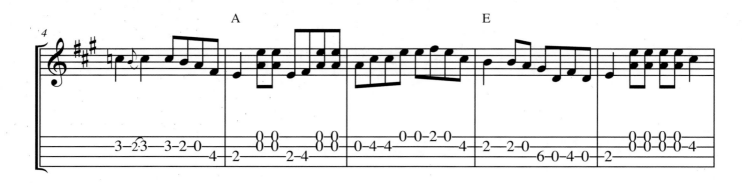

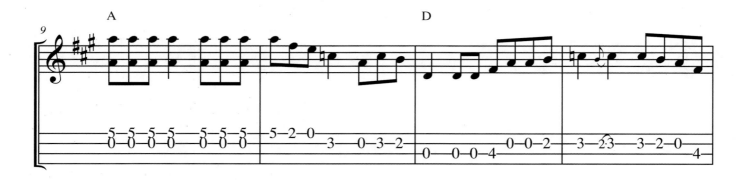

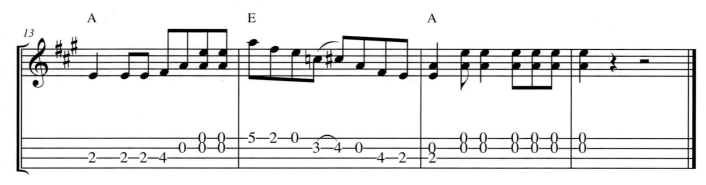

On and On - Bill Monroe

Source: The Music of Bill Monroe MCA Boxed Set - This 1954 vocal trio features guitarist Jimmy Martin and fiddler Charlie Cline. The diamond shaped symbols in measures 8 and 10 indicate these notes should be played as harmonics at the 12th fret. This is an example of Monroe at his most playful and creative. Compare this solo to *The First Whippoorwill*.

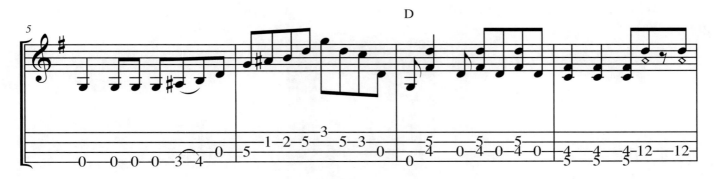

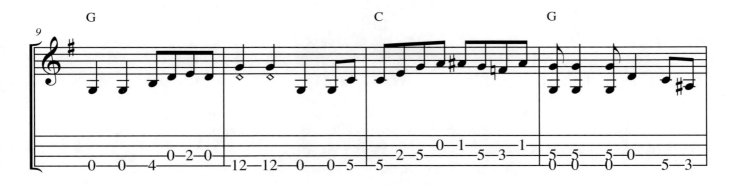

Conclusion

Congratulations on completing this study of Bill Monroe's mandolin style. This volume should give you greater understanding of Monroe's genius as a mandolin player. I tried to write the book I always wanted but couldn't find. Look for other mandolin titles from Mel Bay Publications especially Todd Collin's collection of Monroe instrumentals: 25 Bill Monroe Favorites MB99962:

As Bill Monroe is commonly lauded as "the father of bluegrass music," his tunes are standard repertoire and should be studied and memorized by any serious student of bluegrass. This book is a collection of transcriptions in notation and tablature taken from classic instrumentals recorded over a span of 40 years, from the early 1940s to the early 1980s. It functions as a "fake book" for bluegrass students to learn the original melody or to study Monroe's playing style. The melodies were played by mandolin, fiddle, twin fiddles, or triple fiddles, and are grouped accordingly. Generally included with the fiddle melody is a transcription of the mandolin break. These transcriptions, along with the discography, will be an important resource for any student of bluegrass music.

Here are several books about Monroe you may want to look for:
"The Music of Bill Monroe," Neil Rosenberg and Charles K. Wolfe, Music in American Life, University of Illinois Press, Urbana and Chicago, 2007.

"Can't You Hear Me Callin': The Life of Bill Monroe, Father of Bluegrass," Richard D. Smith, Da Capo Press, 2000.

Photo by Gerald Jones.

About the Author

Since 1985, Joe Carr has been a music instructor specializing in Bluegrass, Western Swing and Irish music in the Commercial Music program at South Plains College in Levelland, Texas. He is a director for Camp Bluegrass, a summer residential Music camp in its 25th year (2011.)

In 1977, Joe joined the internationally known *Country Gazette* bluegrass band with banjo player Alan Munde and bluegrass legend Roland White. Joe appeared on three group albums, a solo album and numerous other recorded projects during his seven-year tenure with the band. In the 1990s, Carr and Munde formed a duo that toured extensively throughout the U.S., Canada and England and recorded two albums for Flying Fish/Rounder Records.

Joe has developed and appeared in over thirty instructional music videos for Mel Bay Publications and Texas Music & Video. He has written many instructional book/CD combinations for Mel Bay and has a growing number of DVDs available. Included are diverse titles such as *Western Swing Fiddle* MB20289BCD, *Mandolin Gospel Tunes* MB20554BCD and *School of Country Guitar* MB21645BCD.

Joe is a regular columnist for *Flatpicking Guitar Magazine* and *Mandolin Magazine*. He is the editor for Mel Bay's webzine Mandolin Sessions. melbay.com/mandolinsessions

In 1996, the Texas Tech University Press published *Prairie Nights to Neon Lights: The Story of Country Music in West Texas* by Carr and Munde. Joe can be seen and heard at acousticmusician.com/JoeCarr.html.